Sports Illustrated KIDS

STARS OF SPORTS

KLAY THOMPSON

BASKETBALL SHARPSHOOTER

■■ by Matt Chandler

CAPSTONE PRESS
a capstone imprint

Capstone Captivate is published by Capstone Press, an imprint of Capstone.
1710 Roe Crest Drive
North Mankato, Minnesota 56003
www.capstonepub.com

Library of Congress Cataloging-in-Publication Data is available on the Library of Congress website.
ISBN: 978-1-4966-8382-3 (hardcover)
ISBN: 978-1-4966-8433-2 (eBook PDF)

Summary: Klay Thompson's skill with a basketball runs in the family. His father was drafted into the NBA in 1978. But it's Klay's own star qualities that shine as he plays for the Golden State Warriors. Known for his shooting ability, Thompson has helped his team win big. Find out more about his career moments and behind-the-scenes facts in this electric biography in the Stars of Sports series.

Image Credits
Associated Press: Ben Margot, 5, Jeff Chiu, 13, Marcio Jose Sanchez, 28, Tony Avelar, 27; Newscom: Cal Sport Media/Louis Lopez, 8, 9, Icon SMI/John McDonough, 7, Icon SMI/Ric Tapia, 10, Reuters/Mike Stone, 16, TNS/Jose Carlos Fajardo, 23, USA Today Sports/Cary Edmondson, cover; Shutterstock: EFKS, 1; Sports Illustrated: Al Tielemans, 17, 22, Erick W. Rasco, 14, 25, John W. McDonough, 15, 19, 21, Robert Beck, 24

Editorial Credits
Editor: Gena Chester; Designer: Sarah Bennett; Media Researcher: Eric Gohl; Production Specialist: Laura Manthe

All internet sites appearing in back matter were available and accurate when this book was sent to press.

Direct Quotations
Page 12, "I think I'm ready . . ." Vince Grippi, "WSU's Klay Thompson Declares Early for NBA Draft," April 18, 2011, https://www.seattletimes.com/sports/wsu-cougars/wsus-klay-thompson-declares-early-for-nba-draft/
Accessed January 10, 2020.

Page 12, "With the eleventh pick . . ." Golden State Warriors, "Behind the Scenes of the 2011 NBA Draft with Klay Thompson," https://www.youtube.com/watch?v=8SoOwnEX6OE
Accessed January 10, 2020.

Printed in the United States of America.
PA117

TABLE OF CONTENTS

Glossary terms are **BOLD** on first use.

RECORD BREAKER

The Golden State Warriors were up 35 points over the Indiana Pacers. There were less than three minutes left in the third quarter. The Warriors' home crowd was on its feet. Then, history was made. Andre Iguodala brought the ball up court. He spotted Klay Thompson on the baseline and delivered a clean bounce pass. Thompson caught the ball and launched a three-pointer. The shot was good!

The basket gave Thompson 60 points for the game. A lot of players have scored 60 points in a game. Thompson became the first player in the National Basketball Association (NBA) to score 60 in under 30 minutes of playing time! This game showcased Thompson as one of the best shooters in the NBA!

Klay Thompson shoots a three-pointer ⟩⟩⟩ at the end of the third quarter of his 60-point game in 2016.

CHAPTER ONE

FAMILY MATTERS

Klay Thompson was **destined** to be a professional athlete. Klay grew up in the shadow of his father, Mychal. Mychal Thompson was a superstar, playing mostly with the Portland Trail Blazers and Los Angeles Lakers. Klay's mom, Julie, was a college volleyball player. Klay and his brothers, Trayce and Mychel, were raised to be **competitors**. All three boys went on to play professional sports. Mychel spent six years playing professional basketball. Trayce played as an outfielder in Major League Baseball. Then there was Klay. He loved basketball from an early age.

Like Father, Like Son

Klay Thompson likes to win. It's what drives him as an NBA player. It is also what drove his dad. The two superstars had career paths that were very similar. Both were **drafted** in the first round of the NBA Draft and named to the NBA All-**Rookie** First Team. They are the only father-son duo in history to each win back-to-back championships!

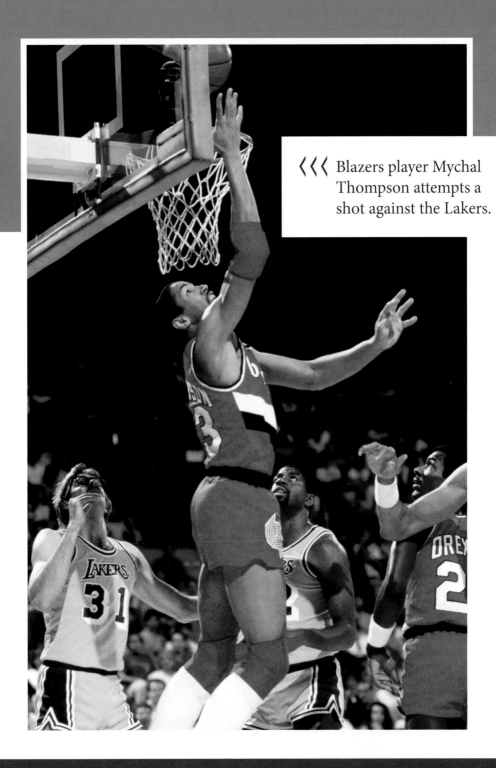

⟨⟨⟨ Blazers player Mychal Thompson attempts a shot against the Lakers.

HIGH SCHOOL HOOPS

Thompson was raised in Oregon. His family moved to California when Klay was about to start high school. He went to Santa Margarita Catholic High School from 2004 to 2008. His high school coach, Jerry DeBusk, helped develop his game. Outside of school, Thompson's dad was his closest **mentor**. But he had other mentors too. His dad stayed in touch with his former team, the Lakers. That meant Klay got to shoot around with Laker all-star Kobe Bryant!

>>> Thompson shoots over a
defender in a high school
basketball game.

Being surrounded by so many great coaches and
mentors helped Thompson improve his game in high
school. He finished his high school career winning
the Division III California State Championship.

CHAPTER TWO

COLLEGE BALLER

Some schools with famous basketball teams wanted to give Thompson **scholarships**. Michigan, Notre Dame, and Minnesota were all interested in him. In the end, he decided to play for Washington State University (WSU).

〉〉〉 Thompson played at Washington State for three seasons.

Thompson shined in his first three seasons at WSU. He started all 33 games his first year. Thompson has always been known for his shooting. That first year, he led the Cougars in free throws and three-point shots. He averaged 12.5 points per game.

Over the next three seasons, Thompson started in 95 games. He ranks at the top of most all-time offensive categories at WSU.

TIME TO GO PRO

Thompson played three years at WSU before entering the NBA Draft. At the time, he said, "I think I'm ready to play at the next level."

He was an early second-round pick. On June 23, 2011, with his parents by his side, Thompson watched NBA Commissioner David Stern speak at the podium.

"With the eleventh pick in the 2011 NBA Draft, the Golden State Warriors select Klay Thompson, from Washington State University." For Thompson, his lifelong dream had come true!

FACT

Living in California, Thompson loved to skateboard. Today, his NBA **contract** bans him from skateboarding, to avoid injury.

<<< Golden State Warriors draft pick Klay Thompson

Five months after the draft, Thompson signed his first pro contract. He was a Golden State Warrior! Thompson thought he'd be a bench player for the first few years of his career and come off the bench to spark the offense with his playmaker skills and long-range shot.

But Golden State believed it had a superstar. Thompson started 111 games in his first two seasons. The Warriors had the start of an unstoppable offense!

⟩⟩⟩ Klay Thompson dribbles around his Brooklyn Nets defender.

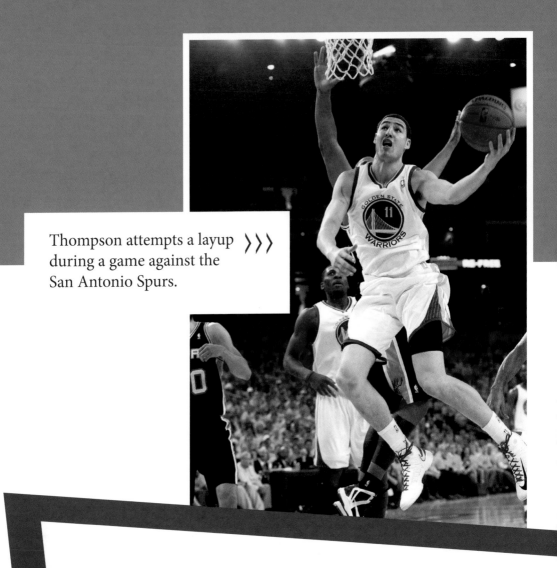

Thompson attempts a layup ⟩⟩⟩ during a game against the San Antonio Spurs.

Pressure to Perform

Thompson is one of several players who have shined in the footsteps of their NBA dads. The Sacramento Kings' head coach, Luke Walton, is the son of Celtics legend Bill Walton. Luke won two titles with the Los Angeles Lakers. Steph Curry has three NBA titles and two MVP Awards—more than his dad, Dell, who played 16 years in the NBA.

HOT HAND

Thompson entered the NBA with a **reputation** as a player who could shoot from anywhere on the floor. In his second season with the Warriors, he proved that to be true. He had a huge season, starting all 82 games. In the playoffs, he averaged more than 15 points per game.

Thompson drives toward the hoop in the 2013 Western Conference quarterfinal playoff series. 〉〉〉

Golden State lost Game One of the Western Conference Semifinals to the San Antonio Spurs in double overtime. Thompson didn't hit a single three-pointer in Game One. In Game Two, he stepped up. Thompson buried eight of nine three-point shots. He scored 34 points to lead the Warriors to the win. It was the highest-scoring playoff game of his young career.

GOLDEN GROWTH

Thompson has gotten better each season with Golden State. One of the best things about him early on was his health. Other teammates missed games with injuries. Thompson showed he could play every game. Through his first eight seasons, he averaged almost 78 games per season.

Thompson makes the other players on his team better. He often draws two defenders to try and stop him when he has the ball. This gives players such as Steph Curry more space to shoot. In Curry's first three years in the league, he never led the NBA with made three-point shots. Once Thompson became a full-time starter, that changed. Curry led the NBA for the next five years in a row!

<<< Thompson shoots a layup during a 2014 game against the Los Angeles Clippers.

Scoring Machine

An NBA quarter is 12 minutes long. If a team is lucky, it will have the ball for six minutes. So for a player to score 37 points in a single quarter is amazing. Thompson did just that in 2015 against the Sacramento Kings. He made 13 of 13 shots. He outscored the entire Sacramento Kings team 37–22 in the first quarter!

CHAPTER FOUR

NBA CHAMPION!

When Golden State reached the 2015 NBA Finals, it was the longest season Thompson had ever played. Game One of the Finals marked the 106th game of the season. Some fans wondered if Thompson and his teammates would have enough left to take down LeBron James and the Cleveland Cavaliers. It didn't take long for Thompson to show people he could. He poured in 21 points and added six rebounds in Game One. The Warriors won the game 108–100.

Thompson raised the bar in Game Two. He scored 34 points in a two-point loss that tied the series. The Warriors went on to win the series in six games. Thompson was an NBA Champion!

>>> The Warriors drafted Steph Curry (left) in 2009. He's played with Klay Thompson since Thompson joined the team in 2011.

FACT

Thompson and teammate Steph Curry earned the nickname "The Splash Brothers" for their three-point shooting.

KING OF THE PLAYOFFS

Thompson has beaten NBA defenses with his shooting during the regular season. But superstars are measured by how they do in the playoffs. Thompson has shown he is an **elite** postseason player.

The Warriors' 2015–2016 playoff run was Thompson's best postseason. In 24 games, he averaged more than 24 points per game.

〉〉〉 Thompson takes a jumpshot in a 2015 game against the Philadelphia 76ers.

《《《 Thompson reacts after scoring a three-point shot in a 2016 game against the Oklahoma City Thunder.

The Warriors faced the Oklahoma City Thunder in Game Six of the Western Conference Finals. They were the away team and close to losing. Then, Thompson took over.

With five minutes left in the game, the Thunder led by seven points. Thompson took a pass from Draymond Green. He launched a long three-point shot. It banked off the backboard into the net. With the shot, Thompson set the NBA record for most three-pointers in a playoff game! He finished the game with 11 from long range and 41 points overall. The Warriors won. They went on to win Game Seven and returned to the NBA Finals.

DYNASTY

In the second half of the 2010s, the Warriors were an NBA **dynasty**. Steph Curry. Kevin Durant. Draymond Green. Klay Thompson. With so much talent, it might have been easy for Thompson to be overshadowed. Luckily, he wasn't.

〉〉〉 Thompson gets the rebound in a 2019 regular season game against the Los Angeles Lakers.

<<< Thompson makes a drive to the basket against his Toronto Raptors defender in Game One of the 2019 NBA Finals.

In the 2019 Finals, Thompson averaged 26 points per game against the Toronto Raptors' defense. He also played hard defense. He grabbed 24 rebounds and four steals over the series. In Game Six, he scored 30 points. The Raptors won Game Six and the series, but Thompson showed he led the Warriors' team of superstars.

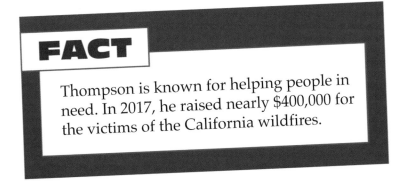

FACT

Thompson is known for helping people in need. In 2017, he raised nearly $400,000 for the victims of the California wildfires.

CHAPTER FIVE
THE FUTURE FOR KLAY

The clock showed two minutes left in the third quarter of Game Six of the 2019 NBA Finals. The Warriors were protecting a slim three-point lead over the Toronto Raptors. Steph Curry picked up a loose ball and raced down the court. He lobbed a pass ahead to Thompson. The big man went up for the dunk, and Raptors guard Danny Green delivered a hard foul. Thompson fell to the court. He clutched his left knee. He had torn his **ACL**. Thompson's season was over, and his future was in doubt.

Recovering from an ACL tear can take an entire year. Some players never really recover. The Warriors weren't worried. They decided to show their confidence in Thompson. Just two weeks after his injury, they signed the superstar to a new contract. The deal was worth $190 million over five seasons.

》》》 The referee calls a foul on Danny Green (14) as Thompson clutches his knee. Thompson had surgery to repair his torn ACL in July that same year.

WHAT'S TO COME?

Klay Thompson collected three NBA titles before he turned 30. He was named to the NBA All-Star team five times. He won an Olympic gold medal. He was a key part of one of the biggest NBA dynasties. What's next? More titles? The Hall of Fame? Only time will tell if he will go down as one of the best to ever play the game!

TIMELINE

1990 Klay Alexander Thompson is born on February 8 in Los Angeles, California

2008 Commits to Washington State University

2009 Thompson collects the first of his three gold medals for international play at the U-19 World Championships

2011 Golden State Warriors select Thompson with the 11th overall pick in the NBA Draft

2012 Named to the NBA All-Rookie First Team

2015 Sets NBA record for most points scored in a quarter

2015 Wins the first of three NBA titles with the Warriors

2016 Thompson earns his first Olympic gold medal as a member of Team USA

2017 Wins second NBA title with the Warriors

2018 Wins third NBA title with the Warriors

2019 Signs a five-year, $190 million contract to stay with Golden State

GLOSSARY

ACL (AY-SEE-EL)—a key ligament in the knee that helps stabilize it; an ACL tear is a common injury among athletes

COMPETITOR (kuhm-PE-tuh-tuhr)—a person who is trying to win in a sport or game

CONTRACT (KAHN-trakt)—an agreement between people stating the terms by which one will work for the other

DESTINED (DES-tuhnd)—something that was bound to happen

DRAFTED (DRAFT-id)—chosen to join a sports organization or team

DYNASTY (DYE-nuh-stee)—a team that wins multiple championships over a period of several years

ELITE (i-LEET)—describes players who are among the best in the league

MENTOR (MEN-tur)—a person who helps and guides someone with less experience

REPUTATION (rep-yuh-TAY-shuhn)—a person's character as judged by other people

ROOKIE (RUK-ee)—a first-year player

SCHOLARSHIP (SKOL-ur-ship)—money given to a student to pay for school

READ MORE

Bryant, Howard. *Legends: The Best Players, Games, and Teams in Basketball.* New York: Philomel Books, 2017.

Chandler, Matt. *Pro Basketball Records: A Guide for Every Fan.* North Mankato, MN: Compass Point Books, 2019.

Mikoley, Kate. *Basketball: Stats, Facts, and Figures. Do Math with Sports Stats!* New York: Gareth Stevens Publishing, 2018.

INTERNET SITES

Golden State Warriors
www.espn.com/nba/team/_/name/gs/golden-state-warriors

Naismith Memorial Basketball Hall of Fame
www.hoophall.com

National Basketball Association
www.nba.com

INDEX